THE LITTLE BOOK OF JAM TIPS

THE LITTLE BOOK OF JAM TIPS

ANDREW LANGLEY

A.
Absolute Press

First published in Great Britain in 2011 by
Absolute Press
Scarborough House, 29 James Street West
Bath BA1 2BT, England
Phone 44 (0) 1225 316013 **Fax** 44 (0) 1225 445836
E-mail info@absolutepress.co.uk
Web www.absolutepress.co.uk

A catalogue record of this book is available
from the British Library

ISBN 13: 9781906650636

Printed and bound in Malta on behalf of Latitude Press

‘I got the blues thinking of the future,
so I left off and made some marmalade.
It’s amazing how it cheers one up to shred
oranges and scrub the floor.’

D.H. Lawrence (1885–1930)
British novelist and poet

1

Jam is a preserve. It preserves fruit and other produce because we artificially boost the sugar content. Sugar discourages the growth of microbes by drawing moisture out of the fruit's cells.

So remember: **it is vital to use the correct proportion of sugar to fruit** in all jam recipes.

2

Appreciate **pectin,** the second crucial ingredient in jams. It occurs naturally in most fruits, and is drawn together by the action of the sugar and the evaporation of water through boiling. The glory of pectin is that it

makes the jam gel,

and give it that firmness and translucence which we all love.

3

Buy yourself a good solid preserving pan.

It should be large, wide and fairly shallow in order to help the evaporation process. A thick bottom aids heat distribution and protects against burning. Avoid aluminium pans, as these can be corroded by fruit acids, and get something in stainless steel.

4

A long-handled wooden spoon is needed for stirring – the longer the handle, the less likely it is that you'll be splashed with boiling jam. A spoon with a straight edge at the tip is extra useful for scraping sugary fruity gunge off the the bottom of the pan.

5

You can make perfectly good jam without

a jam thermometer –

but **life is much easier with one.**

This will show you exactly when the mixture has reached its setting point (a temperature of around 105°C), and spares you a lot of guesswork. Remember to sterilise the thermometer every time before use.

6

It is vital to wash and sterilise all jars and bottles

before filling them. This wipes out harmful microbes inside. The simplest method is to put them (with their lids off) on a baking tray, put the tray in a cold oven and heat to about 110°C for 20 minutes. More wastefully, you can put them in the dishwasher on its hottest setting.

7

You can also sterilise your jars chemically,

using the kind of sterilising tablets recommended for winemakers. Put a tablet in each jar, top up with water and leave for the time specified on the packet. Afterwards, thoroughly rinse with clean water to avoid the risk of a faint aftertaste spoiling your jam.

8

If possible, **use slightly underripe fruit for jam-making.**

It is at this stage that fruit tends to have the highest content of pectin and acid, which helps the gelling process. The higher the pectin levels, the more sugar can be set with the fruit – and the longer the result will last.

9

Some fruits are naturally higher in pectin and acid than others.

These include blackcurrants, redcurrants, gooseberries, plums, damsons and quinces. By contrast, strawberries, raspberries, pears, cherries and blackberries have much lower pectin levels.

10

How do you ensure there's enough pectin in your jam mixture? One way, of course, is to mix high- and low-pectin fruits together. Another is to add a citric acid (try lemon juice or lemon slices). The acid helps to release the pectin from the fruit during cooking.

11

In the wrong place, hot jam is sticky, messy stuff.

When you come to potting up your preserves, a wide-mouthed funnel will avoid a lot of grief. Rest it on top of the jar or pot and ladle the jam in neatly, and say goodbye to the misery of jam dribbles down the sides of your jars. The best material, as before, is stainless steel.

12

Strawberry jam: the ingredients.

Well, strawberries, obviously. Garden-grown and unsprayed would be ideal, but at least the fruit should be sound and not quite squidgy. You'll also need the juice of 2 lemons per kg (2lb) of strawberries, to help set, plus 90g (1lb 120z) of sugar per kg of fruit.

13

To clean strawberries and other soft fruit, wipe gently with a cloth. Avoid washing with water. As the great Jane Grigson put it: 'a strawberry that becomes acquainted with water loses its virtue'. In other words, it's likely to go soggy. Remove any 'hulls' (stalks) at this point too.

14

Strawberry jam: the simmering.

Put the strawberries and the lemon juice into the pan. Bring up to boiling point, turn the heat down to low and cook very gently. The main point of this is to extract the pectin. After 30 to 40 minutes the fruit should have reduced slightly and softened.

15

What kind of sugar should you use?

Ordinary granulated is fine, though you may prefer what is classified as 'preserving sugar', which has bigger granules and gives a clearer colour to the jam. Steer clear of 'jam sugar', which has artificial pectin incorporated. The fewer factory chemicals the better.

16

Warm the sugar before adding it to the fruit.

Spread it on a baking tray and put in a low oven for 10 minutes or so. Warm sugar will dissolve more quickly in the fruit mush and help it get back to the boil more quickly. This gives a fresher tasting jam.

17

Strawberry jam: the boiling.

Pour the sugar into the pan and give it a thorough stir. Then whack up the heat so it gets boiling quickly – but make sure the sugar is all dissolved before the boiling starts. You'll know this when its stops feeling gritty as you stir.

18

No thermometer?

Use the 'saucer test' to work out if your jam is at setting point. Put a small blob on a cold saucer. Blow on it, tip the plate, push it with your finger. If the jam goes wrinkly on top and is reluctant to move about, then it's ready.

19

Strawberry jam: the setting.

Keep boiling fast until you've determined that it has reached setting point – using either the thermometer ('Tip 5') or the saucer ('Tip 18'). This should take about 15 minutes if you've got the fruit/sugar quotient right. Mind out for eruptions of scalding jam. When set, turn off the heat immediately.

20

Warm the glass jars before potting.

This will prevent possible disasters when hot jam meets cold glass and cracks it. Put the sterilised and dried jars on a baking tray in a low oven for 10 minutes.

21

Jam pot covers are essential.

They stop microbes and moisture getting in and spoiling the preserve. They also form a vital barrier between the jam and the lid, which may be metal. Acids in the jam could corrode this, causing unpleasant results. Run out of covers? Use greaseproof paper or clingfilm instead.

22

Strawberry jam: the potting.

Leave the jam to cool for up to 30 minutes, then ladle into the pots via a funnel (or ovenproof jug). Leave at least 3mm (⅛ inch) between jar rim and the top of the jam. Put a silicone paper disc on the jam and a cellophane jam pot cover over the top, then screw on the lid tight.

23

No matter how careful you are,
there is bound to be some mess.

Wipe away drips and splodges

on the outside of the jar

with a warm wet cloth and then dry off.

Mucky pots look (and feel) horrid, and the spillage may encourage the growth of mould.

24

Sometimes, a disconcerting scum will form on top of the boiling jam.

This is nothing to worry about. Once the mixture has reached setting point, skim this off with the ladle. Or try the traditional scum dispersant – a knob of butter stirred in.

25

Gooseberries and elderflowers are a classic jam partnership.

Cover 2kg (4lb) of firm gooseberries in water, add 5 elderflower heads tied in a muslin bag and leave to simmer. When the fruit is softish, remove the elderflowers. Add an equal weight of sugar to the gooseberries and boil until set.

26

If your jam won't set,

take affirmative action. Refrain from simply boiling it to death – the sugar will darken and the jam will end up dull in both looks and flavour. Instead, add the juice of a small lemon and stir this in to perk up the pectin levels.

27

Simple marmalade making: part 1.

There are dozens of different ways to make marmalade. Here's one of the easiest. Simmer 1kg (2lb) of washed Seville oranges in 2 litres (4 pints) of water for 2 hours. When cool, chop the peel, discard the pith and retain the pips.

28

Simple marmalade making: part 2.

Put the peel back in the pan with the strained boiled water, plus the juice of one lemon, and the pips tied in a muslin bag. Boil until it reduces by a third (mark the outside of the pan). Then add 1.5kg (3lb) of warmed sugar and boil away to setting point as with jam.

29

To make lemon curd, melt 75g (3oz) of unsalted butter in a pan. Stir in the juice and grated zest from 2 big unwaxed lemons, 100g (4oz) of sugar and 3 well-whisked eggs. Over a low heat, stir gently until it thickens. Put into pots and seal at once. Eat within a couple of months (the challenge is leaving it that long).

30

Fruit cheeses

aren't made of cheese, but they

go brilliantly with cheese.

One of the best is damson cheese. Simmer 2kg (4lb) of damsons gently in 300ml (½ pint) of water, then mash and sieve. Boil down the pulp a bit and, for every 450g (1lb), add 350g (12oz) of sugar. Cook till thick, and pour out to set.

31

Fruit jellies are easy to make

and lovely to look at. Master the basics and you can use any rather tart fruit, such as a mixture of sloes, elderberries, hips, haws and so on. Wash and simmer them, then drain the juice through a sieve or jellybag. Add 450g (1lb) of sugar for each 500ml (1 pint) of juice and boil to set.

32

Three-day marmalade is the orangiest you can get.

Wash and cut the ends off 12 Seville oranges and a lemon, and soak in 1 litre (2 pints) of water overnight. Next day, simmer for 1 hour and leave to cool. On the third day, slice the fruit, put back in with the juice and 1.3kg (2lb 10oz) of sugar to each 500g (1lb). Boil to setting point.

33

Jam with sugar crystals at the top is usually the result of not stirring enough to dissove it all before the mixture starts boiling.

To get rid of sugar crystals,

stand the jar in a saucepan of cold water and very slowly heat (without boiling). This should get rid of the offending crystals.

34

Be content to make jam in small quantities,

rather than giant batches. If you have some left-over fruit, boil it up and pot it. The smaller the amount of fruit, the quicker the jam will be ready. And the quicker you can make it, the fresher the jam will taste.

35

Blackberry or bramble jelly is one of the glories of autumn – but you can make it even better. Include a cooking apple and a handful of red (underripe) blackberries in the mix. These will add all-important pectin for the setting and a certain zing to the flavour.

36

If you find a supply of green (underripe) walnuts, you're lucky.

Make walnut preserve

by shelling and (gently) skinning the nuts, then soaking in water for 5 days. Add the drained walnuts to a reduced syrup of sugar, water and lemon juice, boil for 30 minutes and allow to cool. Boil again, add a couple of cloves and pot.

37

The most sumptuous way to make redcurrant jelly

is without water. Put the redcurrants, stalks and all, into the pan and heat very gently. Equally gently, squash the fruit with a spoon. After about 40 minutes, put to drain through a bag overnight. Mix the juice with an equal weight of sugar and boil hard for 5 minutes.

38

Always scald jelly bags, muslin, sieves, handkerchieves

– or anything else you might employ for straining jelly from cooked fruit. Pour boiling water over it before use. This gives you two advantages – a microbe-free surface, and a wet one. The wetness encourages the juice to drain out of the fruit.

39

Here's an eccentric **grape jam recipe** from France.

Simmer 2 kg (4lb) of green grapes, and squash through a wide-meshed sieve so you get both pulp and juice. Add 100g (4oz) of sugar, plus 3 figs, 1 apple, 1 pear, 1 carrot, a slice of melon (all chopped) and a cinnamon stick. Boil gently until thick and ready to set.

40

If your jam gets mould on top

– either when newly opened, or when opened for a few days – it is still rescuable. Simply scrape off the mouldy top layer with a spoon and discard it. The jam underneath will be unaffected and still edible.

41

The Greeks – naturally – have the

best method for preventing mould on jams

and other preserves. Simply add something alcoholic to the mixture after cooling but before potting. Raki is the obvious choice but, failing that, use a little brandy or whisky.

42

Here are some

classic fruit combinations for jams: melon and ginger; rhubarb and ginger; plum, orange and walnut; blueberry and elderberry; nectarine and raspberry (yes, really); strawberry, rhubarb and cardamom; Seville orange and star anise. Experiment and come up with your own.

43

***Membrillo* is the Spanish version of quince 'cheese'.**

Cut up your quinces, cover with cold water and boil until soft. Drain and mash through a mouli or sieve. Put the purée in the pan with an equal weight of sugar and boil slowly, stirring frequently. When it turns a maroon shade, pour into a greased shallow dish and leave to set.

44

Jam is not just fruity. Chestnut jam uses a staple food from southern Europe. Cook 1kg (2lb) of peeled chestnuts in salted water for 15 minutes. When cool, skin them and whizz to a purée. Add to a syrup of 1kg (2lb) of sugar and 250ml (½ pint) of water with a vanilla pod. Simmer for 30 minutes and pot (removing the pod first).

45

Rose petal jam

sounds – and tastes – ethereal. Gather 225g (8oz) of rose petals (from *rosa eglanteria* if possible). Make a thick syrup of the same weight of sugar and 150ml (¼ pint) of rosewater. Bung in the petals and a dash of orange water and boil in a suitably ethereal manner till setting point is reached.

46

Sweet aubergines?

Sounds crazy, tastes superb. Trim and half-peel 1kg (2lb) of little aubergines, then simmer in salty water for 10 minutes. Drain and add to a syrup of 1kg (2lb) of sugar, 1 litre (2 pints) of water, cloves, ginger and the juice of a lemon. Simmer for one hour, cool and pot in a wide-mouthed jar.

47

Once you've opened a jar of jam, keep it in the fridge.

It will last there for three or four weeks before the microbes take over. Likewise, use up any preserves you make within a year or maybe eighteen months.

48

Jam-making should be a joy.

If you're feeling guilty about that pile of fruit in the fridge and are pushed for time, just do half the recipe. Cook the fruit and strain the juice. When it's cool, just freeze it. You can carry on with the second half of the process another day.

49

Find a cool, dry and dark place to store your jars of jam and and jelly. Constant warmth is not good for preserves. Coupled with damp, it can encourage moulds and worse. Frequent sunlight is almost as bad, as it oxidises the contents of the clear jars, spoiling both the flavour and colour.

50

Always clearly label your jars of jam and preserves.

Fruits can look indistinguishable after a while and it's nice to know what you're eating. So write the main ingredients on the label, plus the date you potted it. That way you will know how long a jar has been on the shelf.

Andrew Langley

Andrew Langley is a knowledgeable food and drink writer. Among his formative influences he lists a season picking grapes in Bordeaux, several years of raising sheep and chickens in Wiltshire and two decades drinking his grandmother's tea. He has written books on a number of Scottish and Irish whisky distilleries and is the editor of the highly regarded anthology of the writings of the legendary Victorian chef Alexis Soyer.

THE LITTLE BOOK OF
BARBECUE
TIPS
ANDREW LANGLEY

THE LITTLE BOOK OF
BEER
TIPS
ANDREW LANGLEY

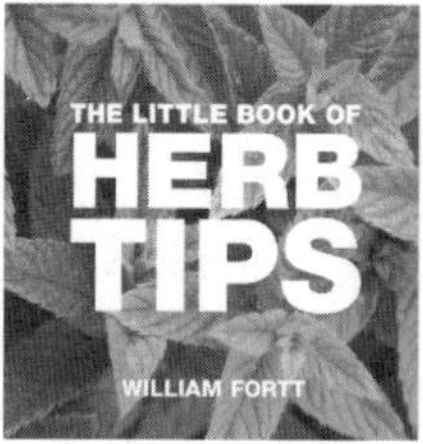
THE LITTLE BOOK OF
HERB
TIPS
WILLIAM FORTT

THE LITTLE BOOK OF
POKER
TIPS

THE LITTLE BOOK OF
GARDENING
TIPS
WILLIAM FORTT

THE LITTLE BOOK OF
CHEFS'
TIPS
RICHARD

THE LITTLE BOOK OF
SPICE
TIPS
ANDREW LANGLEY

THE LITTLE BOOK OF
GOLF
TIPS
PETER FRENCH

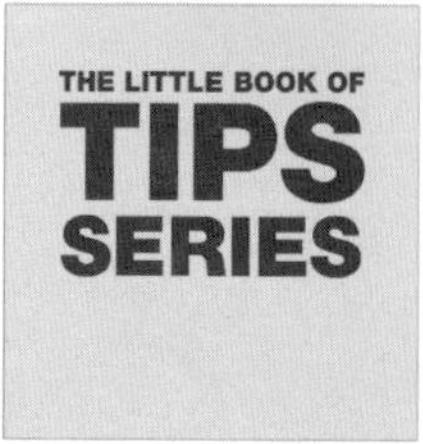
THE LITTLE BOOK OF
TIPS
SERIES

THE LITTLE BOOK OF
CHEESE
TIPS
ANDREW LANGLEY

THE LITTLE BOOK OF
WINE
TIPS
ANDREW LANGLEY

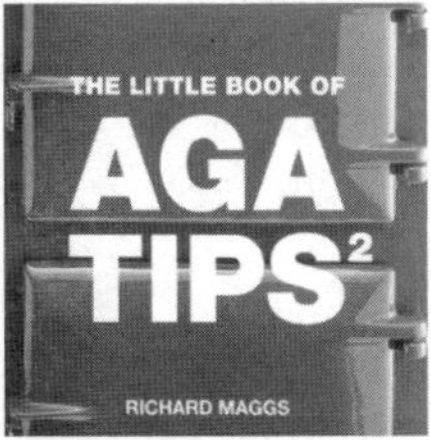
THE LITTLE BOOK OF
AGA
TIPS 2
RICHARD MAGGS

THE LITTLE BOOK OF
COFFEE
TIPS
ANDREW LANGLEY

THE LITTLE BOOK OF
TEA
TIPS
ANDREW LANGLEY

THE LITTLE BOOK OF
AGA
TIPS 3
RICHARD MAGGS

THE LITTLE BOOK OF
AGA
TIPS
RICHARD MAGGS

THE LITTLE BOOK OF
CHRISTMAS
AGA
TIPS
RICHARD MAGGS

RAYBURN
THE LITTLE BOOK OF
RAYBURN
TIPS
RICHARD MAGGS

THE LITTLE BOOK OF
BRIDGE
TIPS
PETER FRENCH

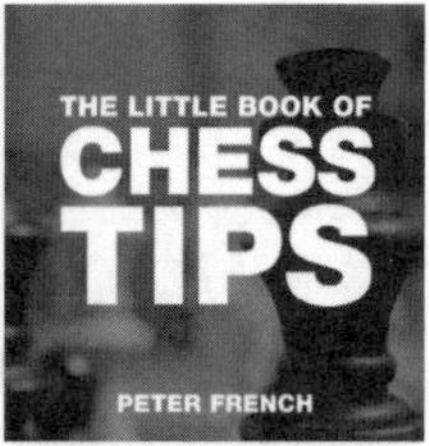
THE LITTLE BOOK OF
CHESS
TIPS
PETER FRENCH

THE LITTLE BOOK OF
FISHING
TIPS
MICK DEVENISH

THE LITTLE BOOK OF
GREEN
TIPS
WILLIAM FORTT

THE LITTLE BOOK OF
KITTEN
TIPS
ANDREW LANGLEY

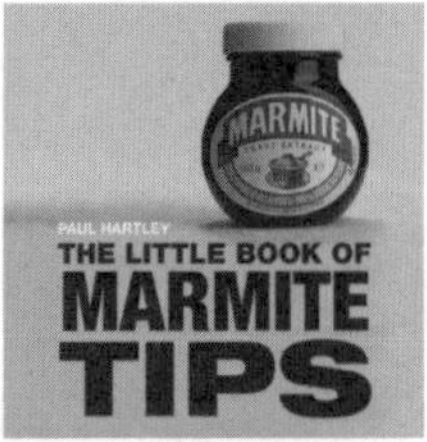
MARMITE
PAUL HARTLEY
THE LITTLE BOOK OF
MARMITE
TIPS

THE LITTLE BOOK OF
PUPPY
TIPS
ANDREW LANGLEY

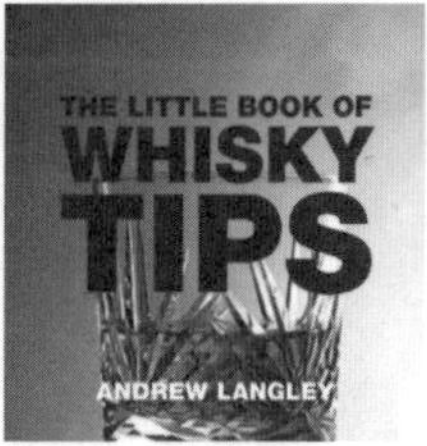
THE LITTLE BOOK OF
WHISKY
TIPS
ANDREW LANGLEY

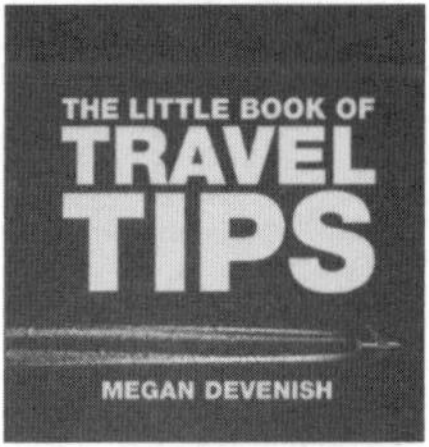
THE LITTLE BOOK OF
TRAVEL
TIPS
MEGAN DEVENISH

Little Books of Tips from Absolute Press

Aga Tips
Aga Tips 2
Aga Tips 3
Backgammon Tips
Barbecue Tips
Beer Tips
Bread Tips
Bridge Tips
Cake Decorating Tips
Cheese Tips
Chefs' Tips
Chess Tips
Chocolate Tips
Christmas Aga Tips
Chutney and Pickle Tips
Cocktail Tips
Coffee Tips
Curry Tips
Fishing Tips
Frugal Tips
Gardening Tips
Golf Tips
Green Tips
Grow Your Own Tips
Herb Tips
Houseplant Tips
Jam Tips
Kitten Tips
Macaroon Tips
Marmite Tips
Olive Oil Tips
Pasta Tips
Poker Tips
Puppy Tips
Rayburn Tips
Spice Tips
Tea Tips
Travel Tips
Whisky Tips
Wine Tips
Vinegar Tips